# HENRI BENDEL

# ₣ASHION
# ⅅESIGNS
## 1915

BROOKLYN MUSEUM OF ART
A BOOK OF POSTCARDS

*Pomegranate*

SAN FRANCISCO

Pomegranate
Box 6099
Rohnert Park, CA 94927

Pomegranate Europe Ltd.
Fullbridge House, Fullbridge
Maldon, Essex CM9 4LE
England

ISBN 0-7649-0626-7
Pomegranate Catalog No. A933

Pomegranate publishes books of
postcards on a wide range of subjects.
Please write to the publisher for more information.

Designed by Elizabeth Key
Printed in Korea
07 06 05 04 03 02 01 00 99 98   10 9 8 7 6 5 4 3 2

To facilitate detachment of the postcards from this book, fold each card along the perforation line before tearing.

# HENRI BENDEL

(1868–1936?) was the founder of one of New York's most influential couture and retail establishments. Born in Louisiana, he emigrated to New York, and by 1896 had established a millinery business on East Ninth Street that soon expanded to include custom-made furs and dresses. He moved the business to Fifth Avenue in 1907 and again to West Fifty-seventh Street in 1912, where he opened a ready-to-wear department. Considered to be one of New York's most exclusive retail establishments, Bendel was for a long time the single largest buyer of Parisian fashion designs. Bendel assembled an extensive collection of sketches to visually document all of their imports as well as the firm's own creations. Many of the sketch designs were copied after Parisian models, several created by the House of Callot Soeurs, and annotated with the name of the garment, the model, the designer, and illustrator.

The Brooklyn Museum of Art has been a leader in the study of costume and textile design since Stewart Culin, the first curator of ethnology from 1903 to 1929, began to build the collection in this area. As research on these collections increased, the Museum Library needed to build its research materials to support study on costume and textiles. In 1942, the Museum Librarians sent a questionnaire to seventy-five designers requesting biographical information and sketches. Subsequently, a major donation was received from the firm of Henri Bendel, which included more than 7,500 sketches of garments made or imported by Bendel from 1912 to 1940, and was supplemented with later gifts of sketches created up through 1950. Today these sketches are used by students, curators, and scholars to understand the influence of French fashion on American design.

Founded in 1823, the Brooklyn Museum of Art Library is the fifth largest art museum library in the nation.

# HENRI BENDEL FASHION DESIGNS 1915

From *Tailored Suits,* Fall 1915

POMEGRANATE   BOX 6099   ROHNERT PARK  CA  94927

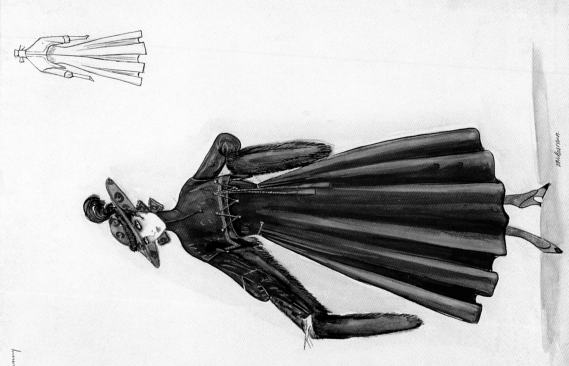

# HENRI BENDEL FASHION DESIGNS 1915

From *Afternoon Gowns,* 1915

POMEGRANATE   BOX 6099   ROHNERT PARK CA 94927

Callot
goffre

# HENRI BENDEL FASHION DESIGNS 1915

From *Tailored Suits,* Spring/Summer 1915

POMEGRANATE BOX 6099 ROHNERT PARK CA 94927

# HENRI BENDEL FASHION DESIGNS 1915

From *Afternoon Gowns,* Spring/Summer 1915

POMEGRANATE   BOX 6099   ROHNERT PARK CA 94927

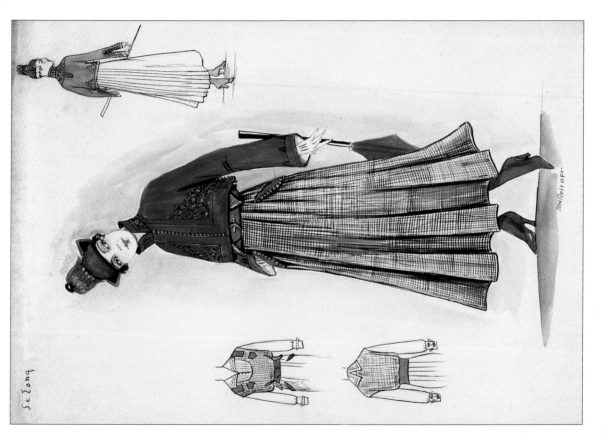

# HENRI BENDEL FASHION DESIGNS 1915

From *Tailored Suits,* Spring/Summer 1915

POMEGRANATE   BOX 6099   ROHNERT PARK CA 94927

Nouvelle qdole
Callot

# HENRI BENDEL FASHION DESIGNS 1915

From *Evening Gowns,* Fall 1915

POMEGRANATE BOX 6099 ROHNERT PARK CA 94927

Indiana
Callot

# HENRI BENDEL FASHION DESIGNS 1915

From *Afternoon Gowns,* Spring/Summer 1915

POMEGRANATE   BOX 6099   ROHNERT PARK CA 94927

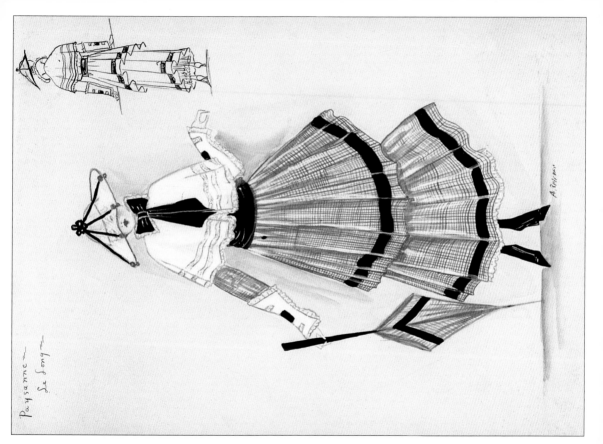

Paysanne —
La Song —

# HENRI BENDEL FASHION DESIGNS 1915

From *Afternoon Gowns,* Spring/Summer 1915

POMEGRANATE   BOX 6099   ROHNERT PARK  CA 94927

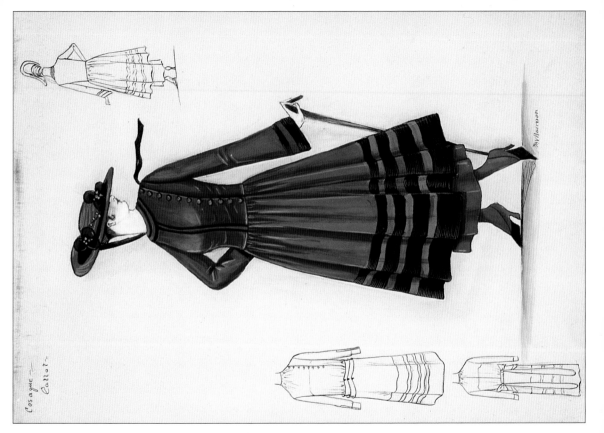

Cosaque —
Callot —

# HENRI BENDEL FASHION DESIGNS 1915

From *Tailored Suits,* Spring/Summer 1915

POMEGRANATE   BOX 6099   ROHNERT PARK CA 94927

# HENRI BENDEL FASHION DESIGNS 1915

From *Afternoon Gowns,* Spring/Summer 1915

POMEGRANATE   BOX 6099   ROHNERT PARK CA 94927

# HENRI BENDEL FASHION DESIGNS 1915

From *Tailored Suits,* Spring/Summer 1915

POMEGRANATE   BOX 6099   ROHNERT PARK CA 94927

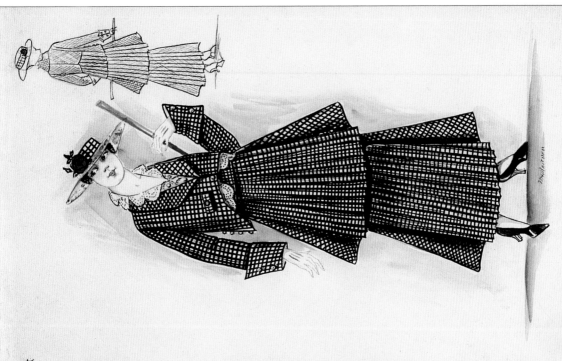

# HENRI BENDEL FASHION DESIGNS 1915

From *Tailored Suits,* Spring/Summer 1915

POMEGRANATE   BOX 6099   ROHNERT PARK CA 94927

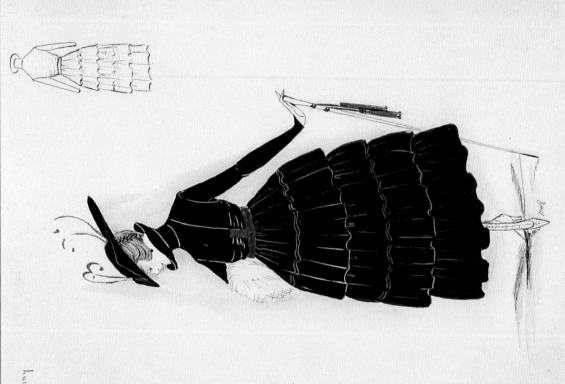

# HENRI BENDEL FASHION DESIGNS 1915

From *Afternoon Gowns,* 1915

POMEGRANATE   BOX 6099   ROHNERT PARK CA 94927

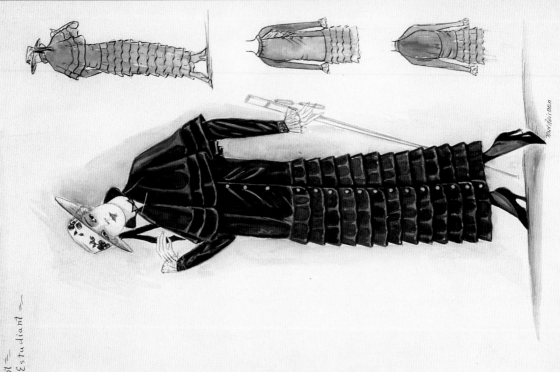

Callot =
Estudiant =

Montleinen

# HENRI BENDEL FASHION DESIGNS 1915

From *Tailored Suits,* Spring/Summer 1915

POMEGRANATE   BOX 6099   ROHNERT PARK CA 94927

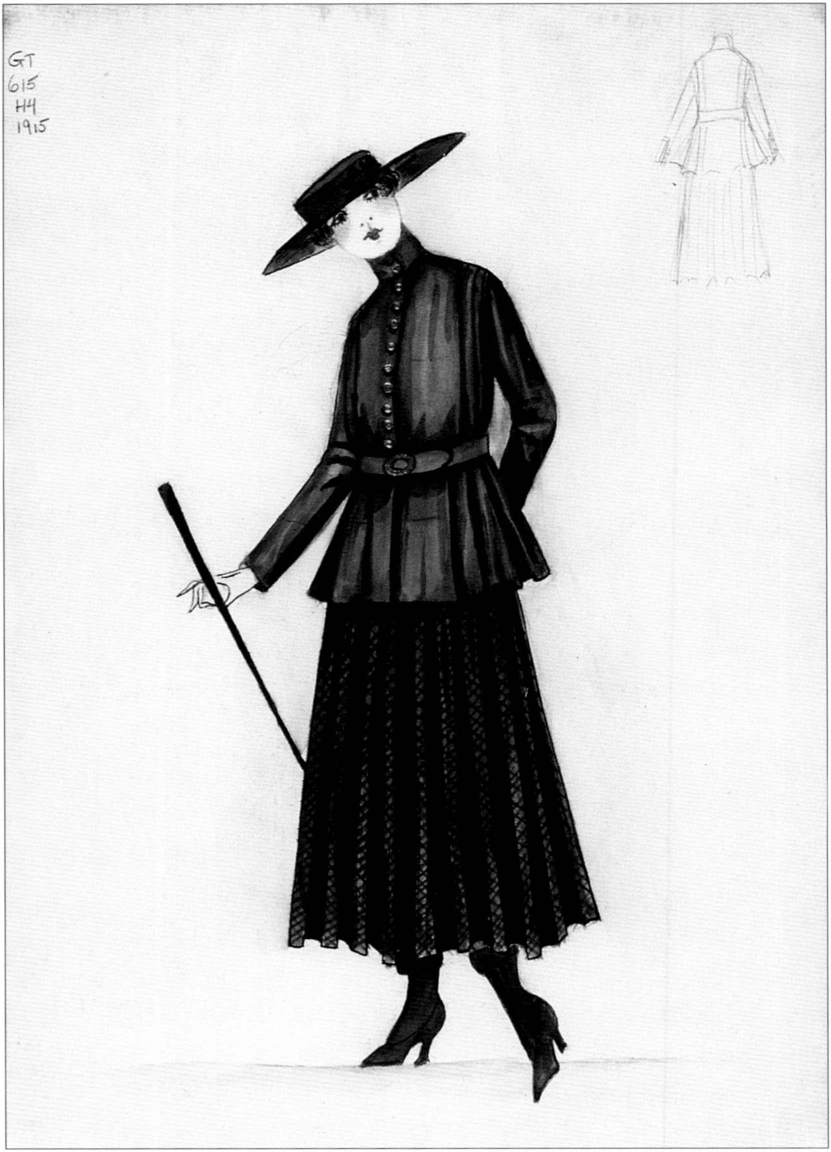
GT
615
H4
1915

# HENRI BENDEL FASHION DESIGNS 1915

From *Tailored Suits,* Fall 1915

POMEGRANATE   BOX 6099   ROHNERT PARK CA 94927

# HENRI BENDEL FASHION DESIGNS 1915

From *Evening Gowns,* Fall 1915

POMEGRANATE   BOX 6099   ROHNERT PARK CA 94927

Callot —
Highlander

# HENRI BENDEL FASHION DESIGNS 1915

From *Tailored Suits,* Spring/Summer 1915

POMEGRANATE   BOX 6099   ROHNERT PARK CA 94927

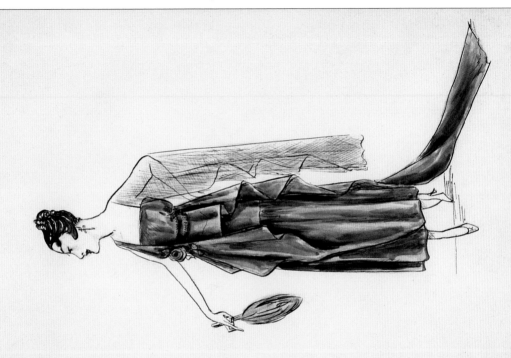

Callot.
Patric:
a,
Gallotin

# HENRI BENDEL FASHION DESIGNS 1915

From *Evening Gowns,* Fall 1915

POMEGRANATE    BOX 6099    ROHNERT PARK CA 94927

# HENRI BENDEL FASHION DESIGNS 1915

From *Afternoon Gowns,* 1915

POMEGRANATE   BOX 6099   ROHNERT PARK CA 94927

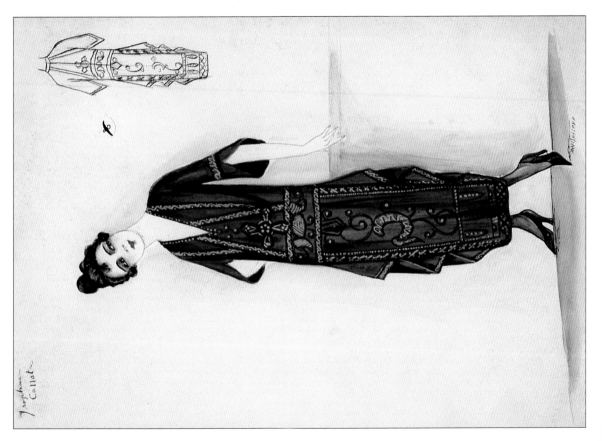

# HENRI BENDEL FASHION DESIGNS 1915

From *Afternoon Gowns,* Spring/Summer 1915

POMEGRANATE BOX 6099 ROHNERT PARK CA 94927

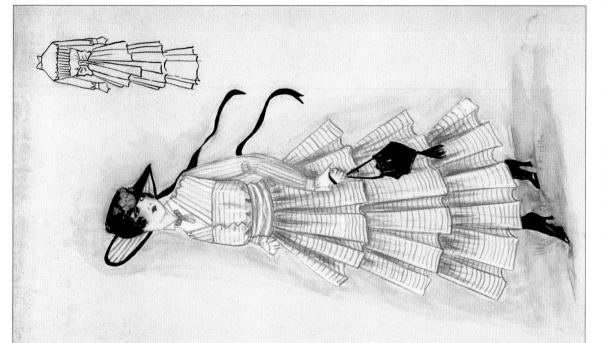

# HENRI BENDEL FASHION DESIGNS 1915

From *Tailored Suits,* Spring/Summer 1915

POMEGRANATE   BOX 6099   ROHNERT PARK CA 94927

*Toujours Aimé*

# HENRI BENDEL FASHION DESIGNS 1915

From *Evening Gowns,* Fall 1915

POMEGRANATE   BOX 6099   ROHNERT PARK   CA   94927

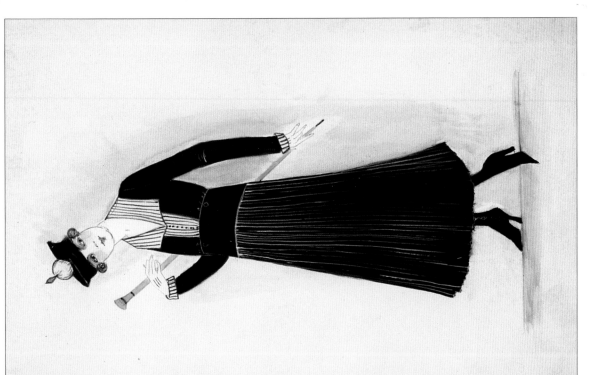

# HENRI BENDEL FASHION DESIGNS 1915

From *Afternoon Gowns,* Spring/Summer 1915

POMEGRANATE    BOX 6099    ROHNERT PARK CA 94927

Cheruit
—Coat—

# HENRI BENDEL FASHION DESIGNS 1915

From *Tailored Suits,* Fall 1915

POMEGRANATE   BOX 6099   ROHNERT PARK CA 94927

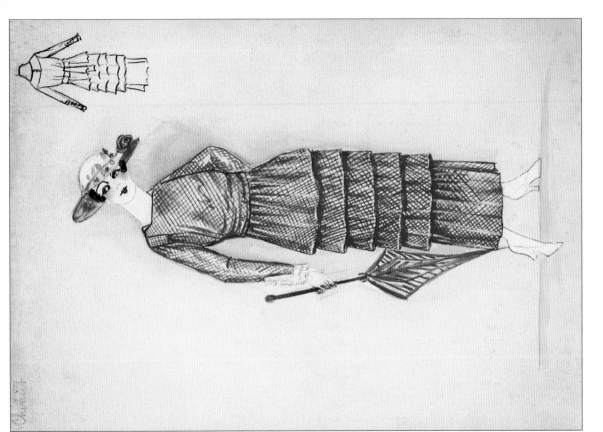

# HENRI BENDEL FASHION DESIGNS 1915

From *Afternoon Gowns,* Spring/Summer 1915

POMEGRANATE   BOX 6099   ROHNERT PARK CA 94927

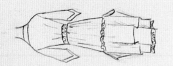

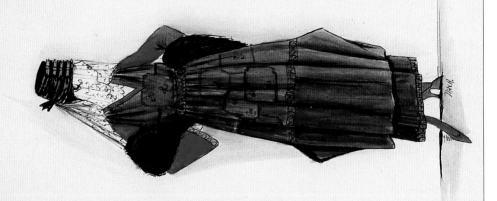

Yoshikito
Callot

HENRI BENDEL FASHION DESIGNS 1915

From *Afternoon Gowns,* 1915

POMEGRANATE  BOX 6099  ROHNERT PARK CA 94927

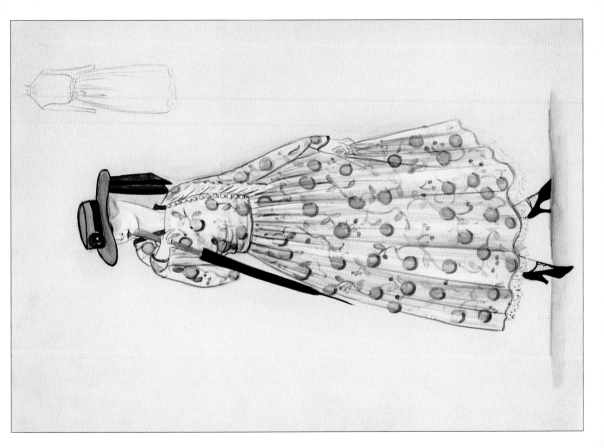

# HENRI BENDEL FASHION DESIGNS 1915

From *Afternoon Gowns,* Spring/Summer 1915

POMEGRANATE   BOX 6099   ROHNERT PARK   CA   94927

Les Platts
Collar

# HENRI BENDEL FASHION DESIGNS 1915

From *Tailored Suits,* Spring/Summer 1915

POMEGRANATE   BOX 6099   ROHNERT PARK  CA  94927

# HENRI BENDEL FASHION DESIGNS 1915

From *Afternoon Gowns,* Spring/Summer 1915

POMEGRANATE BOX 6099 ROHNERT PARK CA 94927

Grande Dans
Callot

# HENRI BENDEL FASHION DESIGNS 1915

From *Afternoon Gowns,* Spring/Summer 1915

POMEGRANATE   BOX 6099   ROHNERT PARK  CA  94927